POEMS

PHILIP LARKIN

Poems

—————

Selected and with an Introduction by
Martin Amis

faber and faber

First published in 2011
by Faber and Faber Ltd
Bloomsbury House
74–77 Great Russell Street
London WC1B 3DA

Typeset by RefineCatch Ltd, Bungay, Suffolk
Printed in England by TJ International Ltd, Padstow, Cornwall

A CIP record for this book
is available from the British Library

ISBN 978-0-571-25810-9

2 4 6 8 10 9 7 5 3

Contents

[v]

Philip Larkin, His Work and Life
by Martin Amis

In the mid-1970s I edited the Weekend Competition in the literary pages of the *New Statesman* (with the judicious assistance of Julian Barnes). One week we threw down the following challenge: contestants were asked to reimagine Marvell's 'To His Coy Mistress' in the style of any modern poet. It was a corpulent postbag: many Gunns, Hugheses, Hills, Porters, Lowells, Bishops, Plaths; and many, many Larkins. First place went to our most trusted star – a reclusive gentleman named Martin Fagg. At the Comp we gave out small cash prizes (Fagg got the maximal fiver), but no prizes are now on offer for guessing which poet he had in mind. This was his opening stanza:

> You mean you *like* that poncy crap
> Where some sex-besotted chap
> Makes love a kind of shopping list?
> Item: two juicy tits. Get pissed!

The lines have a pleasantly hysterical tone (as do many of the best parodies). They also have the virtue of being rich in allusion: allusion to Marvell (the octosyllabic couplet, the poet's fantasised vow to spend two hundred years adoring 'each breast'); and allusion, also, to Larkin. The 'crap'/'chap' rhyme inverts the 'chap'/'crap' rhyme in 'A Study of Reading Habits' (whose anti-literary sullenness Fagg noisily endorses); the poem ends, 'Don't read much now ... Get stewed:/Books are a load of crap.' Now, to transform 'Get stewed' – where '[I]' is

[ix]

torpidly or indeed drunkenly understood – into an emphatic imperative ('Get pissed!') surely veers close to genius. More than this, though, Mr Fagg manages to imitate what is surely inimitable. I read his lines twice, thirty-five years ago, and yet I summoned them without the slightest strain. This is the key to Larkin: his frictionless memorability. To use one of Nabokov's prettiest coinages, he is *mnemogenic*.

Literary crititicism, throughout its long history (starting with Aristotle), has restlessly searched for the Holy Grail of a value system – a way of separating the excellent from the less excellent. But it turns out that this is a fool's errand. Northrop Frye has great fun with the 'evaluative' style in his classic *Anatomy of Criticism* (1957); he takes three poets, Shakespeare, Milton, and Shelley, and 'promotes' and 'demotes' them in all possible permutations, which include:

4. Promoting Shakespeare, on the ground that he preserves an integrity of poetic vision which in the others is obfuscated by didacticism.

5. Promoting Milton, on the ground that his penetration of the highest mysteries of faith raises him above Shakespeare's unvarying worldliness and Shelley's callowness.

6. Promoting Shelley, on the ground that his love of freedom speaks to the heart of modern man more immediately than poets who accepted outworn [. . .]

Etc., etc. (there are eight permutations in all). The 'value' words here, both positive and negative, are in effect mere synonyms for individual preferences. Evaluative criticism is rhetorical criticism: it adds nothing to knowledge; it simply adds to the history of taste. After all, when we say 'Shakespeare is a genius' we are joining a vast concurrence; but we are not quite stating a fact.

How good/great/important/major is Philip Larkin? Instinctively and not illogically we do bow, in these matters, to the verdict of Judge Time. Larkin died twenty-five years ago, and his reputation (after the wild fluctuation in the mid-1990s, to which we will return) looks increasingly secure. And we also feel, do we not, that *originality* is at least a symptom of creative worth. Larkin certainly felt so. In a letter of 1974 he quotes a remark by Clive James – 'originality is not an ingredient of poetry, it is poetry' – and adds, 'I've been feeling that for years.' Larkin's originality is palpable. Many poets make us smile; how many poets make us laugh – or, in that curious phrase, 'laugh out loud' (as if there's any other way of doing it)? Who else uses an essentially conversational idiom to achieve such a variety of emotional effects? Who else takes us, and takes us so often, from sunlit levity to mellifluous gloom? And let it be emphasised that Larkin is never 'depressing'. Achieved art is quite incapable of lowering the spirits. If this were not so, each performance of *King Lear* would end in a Jonestown.

I said earlier that Larkin is easily memorised. Like originality, memorability is of course impossible to quantify. Yet in Larkin these two traits combine with a force that I have not seen duplicated elsewhere. His greatest stanzas, for all their unexpectedness, make you feel that a part of your mind was already prepared to receive them – was anxiously awaiting them. They seem ineluctable, or predestined. Larkin, often, is more than memorable. He is instantly unforgettable.

The following examples are chosen to suggest the variety of registers under Larkin's command. From 'Self's the Man', militant anti-romanticism:

He married a woman to stop her getting away
Now she's there all day,

And the money he gets for wasting his life on work
She takes as her perk
To pay for the kiddies' clobber and the drier
And the electric fire . . .

From 'Aubade', epigrammatic brilliance and truth:

> This is a special way of being afraid
> No trick dispels. Religion used to try,
> That vast moth-eaten musical brocade
> Created to pretend we never die . . .

From 'The Trees', an onomatopoeic prayer for renewal:

> Yet still the unresting castles thresh
> In fullgrown thickness every May.
> Last year is dead, they seem to say,
> Begin afresh, afresh, afresh.

From 'Toads Revisited' ('toad' being Larkin's metaphor for salaried employment), the grimmest and most plangent stoicism:

> What else can I answer,
>
> When the lights come on at four
> At the end of another year?
> Give me your arm, old toad;
> Help me down Cemetery Road.

From 'A Study of Reading Habits', teenage fantasies of power and predation:

> Later, with inch-thick specs,
> Evil was just my lark:
> Me and my cloak and fangs
> Had ripping times in the dark.
> The women I clubbed with sex!
> I broke them up like meringues.

From 'Livings, II', an unusually modernist description – spondee-laden, with almost every syllable stressed – of a nightscape as seen by a lighthouse-keeper:

> By night, snow swerves
> (O loose moth world)
> Through the stare travelling
> Leather-black waters.
>
> [. . .]
>
> Lit shelved liners
> Grope like mad worlds westward.

From 'The Whitsun Weddings', a feeling of epiphanic arrest, as the promise of young lives (or so the poet sees it) goes down the long slide to drudgery:

> [. . .] We slowed again,
> And as the tightened brakes took hold, there swelled
> A sense of falling, like an arrow-shower
> Sent out of sight, somewhere becoming rain.

Then, too, there are the lines that everyone knows and everyone automatically memorises. 'They fuck you up, your mum and dad', 'Sexual intercourse began/In nineteen sixty-three', 'Never such innocence again', 'And age, and then the only end of age', 'What will survive of us is love'. This is a voice that is part of our language.

It is important to understand that Philip Larkin is very far from being a poet's poet: he is something much rarer than that. True, Auden was a known admirer of Larkin's technique; and Eliot, early on, genially conceded, 'Yes – he often makes words do what he wants.' But the strong impression remains that the poets, in general, 'demote' Larkin on a number of grounds: provinciality, lack of ambition, a corpus both crabbed and cramped. Seamus Heaney's misgivings are probably representative: Larkin is 'daunted' by both life and death; he is 'anti-poetic' in spirit; he 'demoralises the affirmative impulse'. Well, these preference-synonyms are more resonant than most, perhaps; but preference-synonyms they remain (still, Heaney is getting somewhere in 'The Journey Back', where the imagined Larkin describes himself as a 'nine-to-five man who had seen poetry'). No: Larkin is not a poet's poet. He is of course a people's poet, which is what he would have wanted. But he is also, definingly, a novelist's poet. It is the novelists who revere him.

Particularly in his longer poems, which resemble Victorian narrative paintings, Larkin is a scene-setting phrasemaker of the first echelon. What novelist, reading 'Show Saturday', could fail to covet 'mugfaced middleaged wives/Glaring at jellies' and 'husbands on leave from the garden/Watchful as weasels' and 'car-tuning curt-haired sons'? In 'The Whitsun Weddings' the fathers of the brides 'had never known/Success so huge and wholly farcical'; in 'To the Sea', immersed in the 'miniature gaiety' of the English littoral, we hear 'The distant bathers' weak protesting trebles' and 'The small hushed waves' repeated fresh collapse . . .'

Many poems, many individual stanzas, read like distilled short stories, as if quickened by the pressure of a larger story, a larger life. The funny and terrrifying 'Mr Bleaney' (a twenty-eight-line poem about the veteran inhabitant of a bedsit) has the amplitude of a novella. And Larkin's gift for encapsulation is phenomenal. Admire this evocation, in 'Livings, III', of the erudite triviality of high-table talk in, as it might be, All Souls, Oxford – and Larkin does it *in rhyme*:

> Which advowson looks the fairest,
> What the wood from Snape will fetch,
> Names for *pudendum mulieris*,
> Why is Judas like Jack Ketch?

'Livings, I' begins: 'I deal with farmers, things like dips and feed.' And after a single pentameter the reader is lucidly present in another life.

Larkin began his career as an exceptionally precocious writer of fiction: he had two pale, promising (and actually very constricted) novels behind him, *Jill* and *A Girl in Winter*, by the age of twenty-five. Twenty-five, and two novels. The reason he gave for abandoning his third (to be called *A New World Symphony*) is, in my view, dumbfoundingly alien. Which brings us to the more fugitive and subliminal component of the fascination Larkin excites in all novelists and in all students of human nature. The poems are transparent (they need no mediation), yet they tantalise the reader with glimpses of an impenetrable self: so much yearning, so much debility;

an eros that self-thwarts and self-finesses. This is what rivets us: the mystery story of Larkin's soul.

Every serious devotee will have read, not only the *Collected Poems* (1988), but also Anthony Thwaite's edition of the *Selected Letters* (1992) and Andrew Motion's *A Writer's Life* (1993). Thus, in our response to Larkin the man, there is a Before and there is an After.

The transition, if you recall, was prodigiously ugly and violent. It began with an attack by the poet Tom Paulin (in the correspondence columns of the *Times Literary Supplement*):

race hatred . . . racism, misogyny and quasi-fascist views . . . For the present, this selection [the *Letters*] stands as a distressing and in many ways revolting compilation which imperfectly reveals and conceals the sewer under the national monument Larkin became.

Here we see, up close, the fierce joys of self-righteousness. You will also notice how quaintly commissarial Paulin's words now sound. For this there is a historical explanation. The *Letters*, and Motion's disaffected *Life*, appeared during the high noon, the manly pomp, of the social ideology we call PC (aka Westernism, Relativism, and – best – Levellism). All ideologies are essentially bovine; and Paulin was simply the leader of the herd, which then duly stampeded.

Next, like a plodding illustration of the domino effect, came the business of 'demotion'. 'Essentially a minor poet,' decided one literary air-sniffer. 'He seems to me more and more minor,' decided another. Yet another, in a piece nobly entitled 'Larkin: the old friend I never liked', suddenly spoke for many when he said that Larkin's poems 'are good – yes – but not *that* good, for Christ's sake'. And so the *trahison* continued, slowly winding down as the ideology lost stamina. Its efforts were of course quite futile. Today, long After, Larkin is back to being what he was Before: Britain's best-loved poet since World War II.

> But if he stood and watched the frigid wind
> Tousling the clouds, lay on the fusty bed
> Telling himself that this was home, and grinned,
> And shivered, without shaking off the dread
>
> That how we live measures our own nature,
> And at his age having no more to show
> Than one hired box should make him pretty sure
> He warranted no better, I don't know.

'Mr Bleaney'

Larkin's life: he was wifeless and childless; he was a nine-to-five librarian, who lived for thirty years in a northern city that smelled of fish (Hull – the sister town of Grimsby). There were in all five lovers: the frail, bespectacled teenager, Ruth; the neurotic 'poetess', Patsy; the religious virgin, Maeve; the 'loaf-haired secretary', Betty (buoyant, matter-of-fact); and overspanning them all, the redoubtable Monica Jones. There were, after a while, no close friends: penpals, colleagues, acquaintances, but no close friends.

What follows is a personal assessment of Larkin's character, and one that reflects a preoccupation that can fairly be described as lifelong. It began in the 1950s, when Larkin was an occasional houseguest at Glanmore Road, Uplands, Swansea. As I now see it, my parents teasingly mythologised Larkin as a paedophobe and skinflint: 'Ooh, don't go near *him*,' my mother used to say, semi-seriously. 'He doesn't like children. And he *hates* giving you your tip.' My 'tip' consisted of three big black pennies; my older brother Philip – Larkin's namesake and godson – got four. The poet unenergetically played his part (the doling out of the pennies was always a grim and priestly ritual). These rare visits continued; he came to Cambridge, London, Hertfordshire. Thinking back, I sense a large, grave, cumbrous yet mannerly figure – and someone distinctively solitary: unattached, unconnected.

I started to read him in my early twenties; we had some professional dealings (he reviewed the odd book for the *Statesman*, and I badgered him for poems); now and then we corresponded; and I spent about half a dozen evenings with him (and others). The closest we came to any kind of intimate exchange was at a drinks party in the late 1970s. We talked about his poem 'Money' (see below). Then I praised him for his courage in learning to drive and buying a car (no other poet I knew would ever go near a steering wheel). Then it went like this:

'You should spend more, Philip. No, really. You've bought the car, and that's good. Now you –'
    'I just wish they wouldn't keep on sending me all these *bills*.'
    'Well it costs a bit to run a car.'
    'I just wish they wouldn't keep sending me all these *bills*.'

If given the slightest encouragement, I might have gone on to suggest, with juvenile impertinence, that he move to London and ... and what? Well, start to live, I suppose. 'He didn't listen,' I said to my father as I drove him home. 'He just went on and on about his bills.'

Larkin died in 1985. And when the *Letters* and the *Life* appeared, almost a decade later, I wrote a long piece in his defence. I should say that I too was struck by Larkin's reflexive, stock-response 'racism', and by his peculiarly tightfisted 'misogyny'. But I bore in mind the simple truth that writers' private lives *don't matter*; only the work matters. A better understanding of the Larkin puzzle would come later. But I felt a premonitory twinge about this, in 1992, when I construed the nature of Larkin's feelings about my father – supposedly his closest friend.

It was always clear to everyone that Kingsley loved Philip with a near-physical passion. Philip probably felt the same, at first (and Kingsley remained his most rousing correspondent). But in his letters to others he seldom mentions my father without sourness. We could adduce envy (sexual and material). Yet there is also a social distaste that feels wholly unworthy: the fastidious suspicion with which the bourgeois regards the bohemian. Kingsley was effectively spurned by the *Letters*; but he never spoke ill of Philip (and continued to read two or three of his poems every night, all the way to his own death in 1995). Still, I remember my father defeatedly saying, on his return from Larkin's funeral, 'It sounds odd, but I sometimes wonder if I ever really knew him.'

No conceivable disclosure could make me demote Larkin's work. But I have come to find his life ever more estranging, and this involves a reevaluation of his character. The long process of assimilating Philip Larkin has been complicated by a process of my own: the ageing process, and what it means.

Nikolai Gogol, who deliberately starved himself to death at the age of forty-two, had this to say, in *Dead Souls*, about the river of time:

[A]s you pass from the tender years of youth into harsh and embittered manhood, make sure you take with you on your journey all the human emotions! Don't leave them on the road, for you will not pick them up afterwards! Old age . . . is terrible and menacing, for it never gives anything back, it returns nothing!

Implicit here, though, is the suggestion that old age does or can give something back: all the human emotions, in the form of memory. The past goes on being present, especially the erotic and romantic past (and a sense of youth remains, vicariously refreshed by one's children). This is an indispensable and, I believe, a near-universal resource.

Now consider the abysmal capitulation of Larkin's letter to Monica Jones in 1956:

Hum. Ha. Ah, don't talk about our lives and the dreadful passing of time. *Nothing* will be good enough to look back on, I know that for certain: there will be nothing but remorse & regret for opportunities missed . . .

This is near-nihilistic: he was thirty-four. And, sure enough, in a letter of 1973 to a fellow poet, Larkin wrote: 'Middle age *is* depressing anyway. The things one tries to forget get bigger and bigger.' This is a psyche trapped in neutral gear: he was fifty-one.

Why did Larkin abandon his third novel? I quote from a letter of 6 July 1953 to the poetess Patsy (described by Kingsley, in a letter to Philip, as 'the most uninterestingly unstable character' he had ever met; she went on to die of alcohol poisoning at the age of forty-nine):

You know, I *can't* write this book: if it is to to be written at all it should be largely an attack on Monica, & I *can't* do that, not while we are still on friendly terms, and I'm not sure it even interests me sufficiently to go on.

The novel 'should' be an attack on Monica? Well of course. What *else* is there to write about?

The attack on Monica was published six months later. But its title was *Lucky Jim* – where Monica is remade as the unendurable anti-heroine, with her barndancer clothes, her mannerisms and affectations, her paraded sensitivity, and her docile-hostile adhesiveness. And *Lucky Jim* was *mentored* by Larkin. In his one concession to gallantry, he made Kingsley change the girl's name – from Margaret Beale to Margaret Peel. The real-life Monica's full name was Monica Margaret Beale Jones.

In 1982 I had dinner with Philip and Monica (and with my brother, father, mother, and stepfather). At the time I found the occasion only mildly bizarre, and wrote about it cheerfully enough in a memoir published in 2000 (though I see that I did describe Monica as 'virile'. This understates the case). Ten years on, I look back at that evening with something close to horror. In Monica's presence, Larkin behaved like the long-suffering nephew of an uncontrollably eccentric aunt. And she was the love of his life.

But that was the kind of life it was. Larkin cleaved to a Yeatsian principle: seek 'perfection of the work rather than perfection of the life' (this is what he means, in 'Poetry of Departures', by 'a life/Reprehensibly perfect').

All the same, there must *be* a life. And it isn't fanciful to surmise that the gauntness of Larkin's personal history (with no emotions, no vital essences, worth looking back on) contributed to the early decline of his inspiration – and, indeed, of his physical instrument. Self-starved, like Gogol, he died at sixty-three.

Larkin is the novelist's poet. He is most definitely *this* novelist's poet. And it is symmetrical, at least, that my final attempt to parse him will be in the form of prose fiction. If I do get anywhere, I may rest assured that I won't be telling his shade anything it doesn't know. Larkin's self-awareness, his internal candour, was merciless. Here are the first and last stanzas of the sixteen-line 'Money'. It shows, as clearly as any poem can, that Larkin siphoned all his energy, and all his love, out of the life and into the work. That he succeeded in this is a tragic miracle; but it is still a miracle.

> Quarterly, is it, money reproaches me:
>> 'Why do you let me lie here wastefully?
> I am all you never had of goods and sex.
>> You could get them still by writing a few cheques.'
>
> [. . .]
>
> I listen to money singing. It's like looking down
>> From long french windows at a provincial town,
> The slums, the canal, the churches ornate and mad
>> In the evening sun. It is intensely sad.

In quality, Larkin's four volumes of verse are logarithmic, like the Richter scale: they get stronger and stronger by a factor of ten. My selection reflects this. From *The North Ship* (1945), one poem out of thirty-two; from *The Less Deceived* (1955), eleven out of twenty-nine; from *The Whitsun Weddings* (1964), twenty-four out of thirty-two; from *High Windows* (1974), twenty-two out of twenty-four. There are four uncollected poems (among them 'Aubade'). I also include two unpublished poems, 'Letter to a Friend about Girls' and (after much hesitation) 'Love Again'. 'Love Again' is there because it is the only poem in which Larkin tries to *account* for what he called his 'neutered' nature. The attempt fails, partly for technical reasons. As he remarked to an ex-colleague, 'It broke off at a point at which I was silly enough to ask myself a question, with three lines in which to answer it.' 'Love Again' concludes:

> . . . but why put it into words?
> Isolate rather this element
>
> That spreads through other lives like a tree
> And sways them on in a sort of sense
> And say why it never worked for me.
> Something to do with violence
> A long way back, and wrong rewards,
> And arrogant eternity.

'Well, of course,' Larkin continued, 'anyone who asks a question by definition doesn't know the answer, and I am no exception. So there we are.'

Dawn

To wake, and hear a cock
Out of the distance crying,
To pull the curtains back
And see the clouds flying –
How strange it is
For the heart to be loveless, and as cold as these.

Coming

On longer evenings,
Light, chill and yellow,
Bathes the serene
Foreheads of houses.
A thrush sings,
Laurel-surrounded
In the deep bare garden,
Its fresh-peeled voice
Astonishing the brickwork.
It will be spring soon,
It will be spring soon –
And I, whose childhood
Is a forgotten boredom,
Feel like a child
Who comes on a scene
Of adult reconciling,
And can understand nothing
But the unusual laughter,
And starts to be happy.

Next, Please

Always too eager for the future, we
Pick up bad habits of expectancy.
Something is always approaching; every day
Till then we say,

Watching from a bluff the tiny, clear,
Sparkling armada of promises draw near.
How slow they are! And how much time they waste,
Refusing to make haste!

Yet still they leave us holding wretched stalks
Of disappointment, for, though nothing balks
Each big approach, leaning with brasswork prinked,
Each rope distinct,

Flagged, and the figurehead with golden tits
Arching our way, it never anchors; it's
No sooner present than it turns to past.
Right to the last

We think each one will heave to and unload
All good into our lives, all we are owed
For waiting so devoutly and so long.
But we are wrong:

Only one ship is seeking us, a black-
Sailed unfamiliar, towing at her back
A huge and birdless silence. In her wake
No waters breed or break.

Going

There is an evening coming in
Across the fields, one never seen before,
That lights no lamps.

Silken it seems at a distance, yet
When it is drawn up over the knees and breast
It brings no comfort.

Where has the tree gone, that locked
Earth to the sky? What is under my hands,
That I cannot feel?

What loads my hands down?

Wants

Beyond all this, the wish to be alone:
However the sky grows dark with invitation-cards
However we follow the printed directions of sex
However the family is photographed under the flagstaff –
Beyond all this, the wish to be alone.

Beneath it all, desire of oblivion runs:
Despite the artful tensions of the calendar,
The life insurance, the tabled fertility rites,
The costly aversion of the eyes from death –
Beneath it all, desire of oblivion runs.

Church Going

Once I am sure there's nothing going on
I step inside, letting the door thud shut.
Another church: matting, seats, and stone,
And little books; sprawlings of flowers, cut
For Sunday, brownish now; some brass and stuff
Up at the holy end; the small neat organ;
And a tense, musty, unignorable silence,
Brewed God knows how long. Hatless, I take off
My cycle-clips in awkward reverence,

Move forward, run my hand around the font.
From where I stand, the roof looks almost new –
Cleaned, or restored? Someone would know: I don't.
Mounting the lectern, I peruse a few
Hectoring large-scale verses, and pronounce
'Here endeth' much more loudly than I'd meant.
The echoes snigger briefly. Back at the door
I sign the book, donate an Irish sixpence,
Reflect the place was not worth stopping for.

Yet stop I did: in fact I often do,
And always end much at a loss like this,
Wondering what to look for; wondering, too,
When churches fall completely out of use
What we shall turn them into, if we shall keep
A few cathedrals chronically on show,
Their parchment, plate and pyx in locked cases,
And let the rest rent-free to rain and sheep.
Shall we avoid them as unlucky places?

Or, after dark, will dubious women come
To make their children touch a particular stone;
Pick simples for a cancer; or on some
Advised night see walking a dead one?
Power of some sort or other will go on
In games, in riddles, seemingly at random;
But superstition, like belief, must die,
And what remains when disbelief has gone?
Grass, weedy pavement, brambles, buttress, sky,

A shape less recognisable each week,
A purpose more obscure. I wonder who
Will be the last, the very last, to seek
This place for what it was; one of the crew
That tap and jot and know what rood-lofts were?
Some ruin-bibber, randy for antique,
Or Christmas-addict, counting on a whiff
Of gown-and-bands and organ-pipes and myrrh?
Or will he be my representative,

Bored, uninformed, knowing the ghostly silt
Dispersed, yet tending to this cross of ground
Through suburb scrub because it held unspilt
So long and equably what since is found
Only in separation – marriage, and birth,
And death, and thoughts of these – for which was built
This special shell? For, though I've no idea
What this accoutred frowsty barn is worth,
It pleases me to stand in silence here;

A serious house on serious earth it is,
In whose blent air all our compulsions meet,
Are recognised, and robed as destinies.

And that much never can be obsolete,
Since someone will forever be surprising
A hunger in himself to be more serious,
And gravitating with it to this ground,
Which, he once heard, was proper to grow wise in,
If only that so many dead lie round.

Toads

Why should I let the toad *work*
    Squat on my life?
Can't I use my wit as a pitchfork
    And drive the brute off?

Six days of the week it soils
    With its sickening poison –
Just for paying a few bills!
    That's out of proportion.

Lots of folk live on their wits:
    Lecturers, lispers,
Losels, loblolly-men, louts –
    They don't end as paupers;

Lots of folk live up lanes
    With fires in a bucket,
Eat windfalls and tinned sardines –
    They seem to like it.

Their nippers have got bare feet,
    Their unspeakable wives
Are skinny as whippets – and yet
    No one actually *starves*.

Ah, were I courageous enough
    To shout *Stuff your pension!*
But I know, all too well, that's the stuff
    That dreams are made on:

For something sufficiently toad-like
    Squats in me, too;
Its hunkers are heavy as hard luck,
    And cold as snow,

And will never allow me to blarney
    My way to getting
The fame and the girl and the money
    All at one sitting.

I don't say, one bodies the other
    One's spiritual truth;
But I do say it's hard to lose either,
    When you have both.

Poetry of Departures

Sometimes you hear, fifth-hand,
As epitaph:
He chucked up everything
And just cleared off,
And always the voice will sound
Certain you approve
This audacious, purifying,
Elemental move.

And they are right, I think.
We all hate home
And having to be there:
I detest my room,
Its specially-chosen junk,
The good books, the good bed,
And my life, in perfect order:
So to hear it said

He walked out on the whole crowd
Leaves me flushed and stirred,
Like *Then she undid her dress*
Or *Take that you bastard*;
Surely I can, if he did?
And that helps me stay
Sober and industrious.
But I'd go today,

Yes, swagger the nut-strewn roads,
Crouch in the fo'c'sle

Stubbly with goodness, if
It weren't so artificial,
Such a deliberate step backwards
To create an object:
Books; china; a life
Reprehensibly perfect.

Deceptions

'Of course I was drugged, and so heavily I did not regain my consciousness till the next morning. I was horrified to discover that I had been ruined, and for some days I was inconsolable, and cried like a child to be killed or sent back to my aunt.' Mayhew, *London Labour and the London Poor*

Even so distant, I can taste the grief,
Bitter and sharp with stalks, he made you gulp.
The sun's occasional print, the brisk brief
Worry of wheels along the street outside
Where bridal London bows the other way,
And light, unanswerable and tall and wide,
Forbids the scar to heal, and drives
Shame out of hiding. All the unhurried day
Your mind lay open like a drawer of knives.

Slums, years, have buried you. I would not dare
Console you if I could. What can be said,
Except that suffering is exact, but where
Desire takes charge, readings will grow erratic?
For you would hardly care
That you were less deceived, out on that bed,
Than he was, stumbling up the breathless stair
To burst into fulfilment's desolate attic.

I Remember, I Remember

Coming up England by a different line
For once, early in the cold new year,
We stopped, and, watching men with number-plates
Sprint down the platform to familiar gates,
'Why, Coventry!' I exclaimed. 'I was born here.'

I leant far out, and squinnied for a sign
That this was still the town that had been 'mine'
So long, but found I wasn't even clear
Which side was which. From where those cycle-crates
Were standing, had we annually departed

For all those family hols? . . . A whistle went:
Things moved. I sat back, staring at my boots.
'Was that,' my friend smiled, 'where you "have your
       roots"?'
No, only where my childhood was unspent,
I wanted to retort, just where I started:

By now I've got the whole place clearly charted.
Our garden, first: where I did not invent
Blinding theologies of flowers and fruits,
And wasn't spoken to by an old hat.
And here we have that splendid family

I never ran to when I got depressed,
The boys all biceps and the girls all chest,
Their comic Ford, their farm where I could be

'Really myself'. I'll show you, come to that,
The bracken where I never trembling sat,

Determined to go through with it; where she
Lay back, and 'all became a burning mist'.
And, in those offices, my doggerel
Was not set up in blunt ten-point, nor read
By a distinguished cousin of the mayor,

Who didn't call and tell my father *There
Before us, had we the gift to see ahead* –
'You look as if you wished the place in Hell,'
My friend said, 'judging from your face.' 'Oh well,
I suppose it's not the place's fault,' I said.

'Nothing, like something, happens anywhere.'

If, My Darling

If my darling were once to decide
Not to stop at my eyes,
But to jump, like Alice, with floating skirt into my head,

She would find no tables and chairs,
No mahogany claw-footed sideboards,
No undisturbed embers;

The tantalus would not be filled, nor the fender-seat
    cosy,
Nor the shelves stuffed with small-printed books for the
    Sabbath,
Nor the butler bibulous, the housemaids lazy:

She would find herself looped with the creep of varying
    light,
Monkey-brown, fish-grey, a string of infected circles
Loitering like bullies, about to coagulate;

Delusions that shrink to the size of a woman's glove,
Then sicken inclusively outwards. She would also
    remark
The unwholesome floor, as it might be the skin of a
    grave,

From which ascends an adhesive sense of betrayal,
A Grecian statue kicked in the privates, money,
A swill-tub of finer feelings. But most of all

She'd be stopping her ears against the incessant recital
Intoned by reality, larded with technical terms,
Each one double-yolked with meaning and meaning's
    rebuttal:

For the skirl of that bulletin unpicks the world like a
    knot,
And to hear how the past is past and the future neuter
Might knock my darling off her unpriceable pivot.

At Grass

The eye can hardly pick them out
From the cold shade they shelter in,
Till wind distresses tail and mane;
Then one crops grass, and moves about
– The other seeming to look on –
And stands anonymous again.

Yet fifteen years ago, perhaps
Two dozen distances sufficed
To fable them: faint afternoons
Of Cups and Stakes and Handicaps,
Whereby their names were artificed
To inlay faded, classic Junes –

Silks at the start: against the sky
Numbers and parasols: outside,
Squadrons of empty cars, and heat,
And littered grass: then the long cry
Hanging unhushed till it subside
To stop-press columns on the street.

Do memories plague their ears like flies?
They shake their heads. Dusk brims the shadows.
Summer by summer all stole away,
The starting-gates, the crowds and cries –
All but the unmolesting meadows.
Almanacked, their names live; they

Have slipped their names, and stand at ease,
Or gallop for what must be joy,
And not a fieldglass sees them home,
Or curious stop-watch prophesies:
Only the groom, and the groom's boy,
With bridles in the evening come.

Here

Swerving east, from rich industrial shadows
And traffic all night north; swerving through fields
Too thin and thistled to be called meadows,
And now and then a harsh-named halt, that shields
Workmen at dawn; swerving to solitude
Of skies and scarecrows, haystacks, hares and pheasants,
And the widening river's slow presence,
The piled gold clouds, the shining gull-marked mud,

Gathers to the surprise of a large town:
Here domes and statues, spires and cranes cluster
Beside grain-scattered streets, barge-crowded water,
And residents from raw estates, brought down
The dead straight miles by stealing flat-faced trolleys,
Push through plate-glass swing doors to their desires –
Cheap suits, red kitchen-ware, sharp shoes, iced lollies,
Electric mixers, toasters, washers, driers –

A cut-price crowd, urban yet simple, dwelling
Where only salesmen and relations come
Within a terminate and fishy-smelling
Pastoral of ships up streets, the slave museum,
Tattoo-shops, consulates, grim head-scarfed wives;
And out beyond its mortgaged half-built edges
Fast-shadowed wheat-fields, running high as hedges,
Isolate villages, where removed lives

Loneliness clarifies. Here silence stands
Like heat. Here leaves unnoticed thicken,

Hidden weeds flower, neglected waters quicken,
Luminously-peopled air ascends;
And past the poppies bluish neutral distance
Ends the land suddenly beyond a beach
Of shapes and shingle. Here is unfenced existence:
Facing the sun, untalkative, out of reach.

Mr Bleaney

'This was Mr Bleaney's room. He stayed
The whole time he was at the Bodies, till
They moved him.' Flowered curtains, thin and frayed,
Fall to within five inches of the sill,

Whose window shows a strip of building land,
Tussocky, littered. 'Mr Bleaney took
My bit of garden properly in hand.'
Bed, upright chair, sixty-watt bulb, no hook

Behind the door, no room for books or bags –
'I'll take it.' So it happens that I lie
Where Mr Bleaney lay, and stub my fags
On the same saucer-souvenir, and try

Stuffing my ears with cotton-wool, to drown
The jabbering set he egged her on to buy.
I know his habits – what time he came down,
His preference for sauce to gravy, why

He kept on plugging at the four aways –
Likewise their yearly frame: the Frinton folk
Who put him up for summer holidays,
And Christmas at his sister's house in Stoke.

But if he stood and watched the frigid wind
Tousling the clouds, lay on the fusty bed
Telling himself that this was home, and grinned,
And shivered, without shaking off the dread

That how we live measures our own nature,
And at his age having no more to show
Than one hired box should make him pretty sure
He warranted no better, I don't know.

Nothing To Be Said

For nations vague as weed,
For nomads among stones,
Small-statured cross-faced tribes
And cobble-close families
In mill-towns on dark mornings
Life is slow dying.

So are their separate ways
Of building, benediction,
Measuring love and money
Ways of slow dying.
The day spent hunting pig
Or holding a garden-party,

Hours giving evidence
Or birth, advance
On death equally slowly.
And saying so to some
Means nothing; others it leaves
Nothing to be said.

Naturally the Foundation will
Bear Your Expenses

Hurrying to catch my Comet
    One dark November day,
Which soon would snatch me from it
    To the sunshine of Bombay,
I pondered pages Berkeley
    Not three weeks since had heard,
Perceiving Chatto darkly
    Through the mirror of the Third.

Crowds, colourless and careworn,
    Had made my taxi late,
Yet not till I was airborne
    Did I recall the date –
That day when Queen and Minister
    And Band of Guards and all
Still act their solemn-sinister
    Wreath-rubbish in Whitehall.

It used to make me throw up,
    These mawkish nursery games:
O when will England grow up?
    – But I outsoar the Thames,
And dwindle off down Auster
    To greet Professor Lal
(He once met Morgan Forster),
    My contact and my pal.

Faith Healing

Slowly the women file to where he stands
Upright in rimless glasses, silver hair,
Dark suit, white collar. Stewards tirelessly
Persuade them onwards to his voice and hands,
Within whose warm spring rain of loving care
Each dwells some twenty seconds. *Now, dear child,
What's wrong*, the deep American voice demands,
And, scarcely pausing, goes into a prayer
Directing God about this eye, that knee.
Their heads are clasped abruptly; then, exiled

Like losing thoughts, they go in silence; some
Sheepishly stray, not back into their lives
Just yet; but some stay stiff, twitching and loud
With deep hoarse tears, as if a kind of dumb
And idiot child within them still survives
To re-awake at kindness, thinking a voice
At last calls them alone, that hands have come
To lift and lighten; and such joy arrives
Their thick tongues blort, their eyes squeeze
        grief, a crowd
Of huge unheard answers jam and rejoice –

What's wrong! Moustached in flowered frocks they
        shake:
By now, all's wrong. In everyone there sleeps
A sense of life lived according to love.
To some it means the difference they could make
By loving others, but across most it sweeps

As all they might have done had they been loved.
That nothing cures. An immense slackening ache,
As when, thawing, the rigid landscape weeps,
Spreads slowly through them – that, and the voice
    above
Saying *Dear child*, and all time has disproved.

For Sidney Bechet

That note you hold, narrowing and rising, shakes
Like New Orleans reflected on the water,
And in all ears appropriate falsehood wakes,

Building for some a legendary Quarter
Of balconies, flower-baskets and quadrilles,
Everyone making love and going shares –

Oh, play that thing! Mute glorious Storyvilles
Others may license, grouping round their chairs
Sporting-house girls like circus tigers (priced

Far above rubies) to pretend their fads,
While scholars *manqués* nod around unnoticed
Wrapped up in personnels like old plaids.

On me your voice falls as they say love should,
Like an enormous yes. My Crescent City
Is where your speech alone is understood,

And greeted as the natural noise of good,
Scattering long-haired grief and scored pity.

Toads Revisited

Walking around in the park
Should feel better than work:
The lake, the sunshine,
The grass to lie on,

Blurred playground noises
Beyond black-stockinged nurses –
Not a bad place to be.
Yet it doesn't suit me,

Being one of the men
You meet of an afternoon:
Palsied old step-takers,
Hare-eyed clerks with the jitters,

Waxed-fleshed out-patients
Still vague from accidents,
And characters in long coats
Deep in the litter-baskets –

All dodging the toad work
By being stupid or weak.
Think of being them!
Hearing the hours chime,

Watching the bread delivered,
The sun by clouds covered,
The children going home;
Think of being them,

Turning over their failures
By some bed of lobelias,
Nowhere to go but indoors,
No friends but empty chairs –

No, give me my in-tray,
My loaf-haired secretary,
My shall-I-keep-the-call-in-Sir:
What else can I answer,

When the lights come on at four
At the end of another year?
Give me your arm, old toad;
Help me down Cemetery Road.

The Whitsun Weddings

That Whitsun, I was late getting away:
    Not till about
One-twenty on the sunlit Saturday
Did my three-quarters-empty train pull out,
All windows down, all cushions hot, all sense
Of being in a hurry gone. We ran
Behind the backs of houses, crossed a street
Of blinding windscreens, smelt the fish-dock; thence
The river's level drifting breadth began,
Where sky and Lincolnshire and water meet.

All afternoon, through the tall heat that slept
    For miles inland,
A slow and stopping curve southwards we kept.
Wide farms went by, short-shadowed cattle, and
Canals with floatings of industrial froth;
A hothouse flashed uniquely: hedges dipped
And rose: and now and then a smell of grass
Displaced the reek of buttoned carriage-cloth
Until the next town, new and nondescript,
Approached with acres of dismantled cars.

At first, I didn't notice what a noise
    The weddings made
Each station that we stopped at: sun destroys
The interest of what's happening in the shade,
And down the long cool platforms whoops and skirls
I took for porters larking with the mails,
And went on reading. Once we started, though,

We passed them, grinning and pomaded, girls
In parodies of fashion, heels and veils,
All posed irresolutely, watching us go,

As if out on the end of an event
    Waving goodbye
To something that survived it. Struck, I leant
More promptly out next time, more curiously,
And saw it all again in different terms:
The fathers with broad belts under their suits
And seamy foreheads; mothers loud and fat;
An uncle shouting smut; and then the perms,
The nylon gloves and jewellery-substitutes,
The lemons, mauves, and olive-ochres that

Marked off the girls unreally from the rest.
    Yes, from cafés
And banquet-halls up yards, and bunting-dressed
Coach-party annexes, the wedding-days
Were coming to an end. All down the line
Fresh couples climbed aboard: the rest stood round;
The last confetti and advice were thrown,
And, as we moved, each face seemed to define
Just what it saw departing: children frowned
At something dull; fathers had never known

Success so huge and wholly farcical;
    The women shared
The secret like a happy funeral;
While girls, gripping their handbags tighter, stared
At a religious wounding. Free at last,
And loaded with the sum of all they saw,
We hurried towards London, shuffling gouts of steam.

Now fields were building-plots, and poplars cast
Long shadows over major roads, and for
Some fifty minutes, that in time would seem

Just long enough to settle hats and say
    I nearly died,
A dozen marriages got under way.
They watched the landscape, sitting side by side
– An Odeon went past, a cooling tower,
And someone running up to bowl – and none
Thought of the others they would never meet
Or how their lives would all contain this hour.
I thought of London spread out in the sun,
Its postal districts packed like squares of wheat:

There we were aimed. And as we raced across
    Bright knots of rail
Past standing Pullmans, walls of blackened moss
Came close, and it was nearly done, this frail
Travelling coincidence; and what it held
Stood ready to be loosed with all the power
That being changed can give. We slowed again,
And as the tightened brakes took hold, there swelled
A sense of falling, like an arrow-shower
Sent out of sight, somewhere becoming rain.

Self's the Man

Oh, no one can deny
That Arnold is less selfish than I.
He married a woman to stop her getting away
Now she's there all day,

And the money he gets for wasting his life on work
She takes as her perk
To pay for the kiddies' clobber and the drier
And the electric fire,

And when he finishes supper
Planning to have a read at the evening paper
It's *Put a screw in this wall* –
He has no time at all,

With the nippers to wheel round the houses
And the hall to paint in his old trousers
And that letter to her mother
Saying *Won't you come for the summer.*

To compare his life and mine
Makes me feel a swine:
Oh, no one can deny
That Arnold is less selfish than I.

But wait, not so fast:
Is there such a contrast?
He was out for his own ends
Not just pleasing his friends;

And if it was such a mistake
He still did it for his own sake,
Playing his own game.
So he and I are the same,

Only I'm a better hand
At knowing what I can stand
Without them sending a van –
Or I suppose I can.

MCMXIV

Those long uneven lines
Standing as patiently
As if they were stretched outside
The Oval or Villa Park,
The crowns of hats, the sun
On moustached archaic faces
Grinning as if it were all
An August Bank Holiday lark;

And the shut shops, the bleached
Established names on the sunblinds,
The farthings and sovereigns,
And dark-clothed children at play
Called after kings and queens,
The tin advertisements
For cocoa and twist, and the pubs
Wide open all day;

And the countryside not caring:
The place-names all hazed over
With flowering grasses, and fields
Shadowing Domesday lines
Under wheat's restless silence;
The differently-dressed servants
With tiny rooms in huge houses,
The dust behind limousines;

Never such innocence,
Never before or since,

As changed itself to past
Without a word – the men
Leaving the gardens tidy,
The thousands of marriages
Lasting a little while longer:
Never such innocence again.

Talking in Bed

Talking in bed ought to be easiest,
Lying together there goes back so far,
An emblem of two people being honest.

Yet more and more time passes silently.
Outside, the wind's incomplete unrest
Builds and disperses clouds about the sky,

And dark towns heap up on the horizon.
None of this cares for us. Nothing shows why
At this unique distance from isolation

It becomes still more difficult to find
Words at once true and kind,
Or not untrue and not unkind.

A Study of Reading Habits

When getting my nose in a book
Cured most things short of school,
It was worth ruining my eyes
To know I could still keep cool,
And deal out the old right hook
To dirty dogs twice my size.

Later, with inch-thick specs,
Evil was just my lark:
Me and my cloak and fangs
Had ripping times in the dark.
The women I clubbed with sex!
I broke them up like meringues.

Don't read much now: the dude
Who lets the girl down before
The hero arrives, the chap
Who's yellow and keeps the store,
Seem far too familiar. Get stewed:
Books are a load of crap.

Ambulances

Closed like confessionals, they thread
Loud noons of cities, giving back
None of the glances they absorb.
Light glossy grey, arms on a plaque,
They come to rest at any kerb:
All streets in time are visited.

Then children strewn on steps or road,
Or women coming from the shops
Past smells of different dinners, see
A wild white face that overtops
Red stretcher-blankets momently
As it is carried in and stowed,

And sense the solving emptiness
That lies just under all we do,
And for a second get it whole,
So permanent and blank and true.
The fastened doors recede. *Poor soul,*
They whisper at their own distress;

For borne away in deadened air
May go the sudden shut of loss
Round something nearly at an end,
And what cohered in it across
The years, the unique random blend
Of families and fashions, there

At last begin to loosen. Far
From the exchange of love to lie
Unreachable inside a room
The traffic parts to let go by
Brings closer what is left to come,
And dulls to distance all we are.

Dockery and Son

'Dockery was junior to you,
Wasn't he?' said the Dean. 'His son's here now.'
Death-suited, visitant, I nod. 'And do
You keep in touch with –' Or remember how
Black-gowned, unbreakfasted, and still half-tight
We used to stand before that desk, to give
'Our version' of 'these incidents last night'?
I try the door of where I used to live:

Locked. The lawn spreads dazzlingly wide.
A known bell chimes. I catch my train, ignored.
Canal and clouds and colleges subside
Slowly from view. But Dockery, good Lord,
Anyone up today must have been born
In '43, when I was twenty-one.
If he was younger, did he get this son
At nineteen, twenty? Was he that withdrawn

High-collared public-schoolboy, sharing rooms
With Cartwright who was killed? Well, it just shows
How much . . . How little . . . Yawning, I suppose
I fell asleep, waking at the fumes
And furnace-glares of Sheffield, where I changed,
And ate an awful pie, and walked along
The platform to its end to see the ranged
Joining and parting lines reflect a strong

Unhindered moon. To have no son, no wife,
No house or land still seemed quite natural.

Only a numbness registered the shock
Of finding out how much had gone of life,
How widely from the others. Dockery, now:
Only nineteen, he must have taken stock
Of what he wanted, and been capable
Of . . . No, that's not the difference: rather, how

Convinced he was he should be added to!
Why did he think adding meant increase?
To me it was dilution. Where do these
Innate assumptions come from? Not from what
We think truest, or most want to do:
Those warp tight-shut, like doors. They're more a style
Our lives bring with them: habit for a while,
Suddenly they harden into all we've got

And how we got it; looked back on, they rear
Like sand-clouds, thick and close, embodying
For Dockery a son, for me nothing,
Nothing with all a son's harsh patronage.
Life is first boredom, then fear.
Whether or not we use it, it goes,
And leaves what something hidden from us chose,
And age, and then the only end of age.

Wild Oats

About twenty years ago
Two girls came in where I worked –
A bosomy English rose
And her friend in specs I could talk to.
Faces in those days sparked
The whole shooting-match off, and I doubt
If ever one had like hers:
But it was the friend I took out,

And in seven years after that
Wrote over four hundred letters,
Gave a ten-guinea ring
I got back in the end, and met
At numerous cathedral cities
Unknown to the clergy. I believe
I met beautiful twice. She was trying
Both times (so I thought) not to laugh.

Parting, after about five
Rehearsals, was an agreement
That I was too selfish, withdrawn,
And easily bored to love.
Well, useful to get that learnt.
In my wallet are still two snaps
Of bosomy rose with fur gloves on.
Unlucky charms, perhaps.

Send No Money

Standing under the fobbed
Impendent belly of Time
Tell me the truth, I said,
Teach me the way things go.
All the other lads there
Were itching to have a bash
But I thought wanting unfair:
It and finding out clash.

So he patted my head, booming *Boy*,
There's no green in your eye:
Sit here, and watch the hail
Of occurrence clobber life out
To a shape no one sees –
Dare you look at that straight?
Oh thank you, I said, *Oh yes please*,
And sat down to wait.

Half life is over now,
And I meet full face on dark mornings
The bestial visor, bent in
By the blows of what happened to happen.
What does it prove? Sod all.
In this way I spent youth,
Tracing the trite untransferable
Truss-advertisement, truth.

Afternoons

Summer is fading:
The leaves fall in ones and twos
From trees bordering
The new recreation ground.
In the hollows of afternoons
Young mothers assemble
At swing and sandpit
Setting free their children.

Behind them, at intervals,
Stand husbands in skilled trades,
An estateful of washing,
And the albums, lettered
Our Wedding, lying
Near the television:
Before them, the wind
Is ruining their courting-places

That are still courting-places
(But the lovers are all in school),
And their children, so intent on
Finding more unripe acorns,
Expect to be taken home.
Their beauty has thickened.
Something is pushing them
To the side of their own lives.

An Arundel Tomb

Side by side, their faces blurred,
The earl and countess lie in stone,
Their proper habits vaguely shown
As jointed armour, stiffened pleat,
And that faint hint of the absurd –
The little dogs under their feet.

Such plainness of the pre-baroque
Hardly involves the eye, until
It meets his left-hand gauntlet, still
Clasped empty in the other; and
One sees, with a sharp tender shock,
His hand withdrawn, holding her hand.

They would not think to lie so long.
Such faithfulness in effigy
Was just a detail friends would see:
A sculptor's sweet commissioned grace
Thrown off in helping to prolong
The Latin names around the base.

They would not guess how early in
Their supine stationary voyage
The air would change to soundless damage,
Turn the old tenantry away;
How soon succeeding eyes begin
To look, not read. Rigidly they

Persisted, linked, through lengths and breadths
Of time. Snow fell, undated. Light
Each summer thronged the glass. A bright
Litter of birdcalls strewed the same
Bone-riddled ground. And up the paths
The endless altered people came,

Washing at their identity.
Now, helpless in the hollow of
An unarmorial age, a trough
Of smoke in slow suspended skeins
Above their scrap of history,
Only an attitude remains:

Time has transfigured them into
Untruth. The stone fidelity
They hardly meant has come to be
Their final blazon, and to prove
Our almost-instinct almost true:
What will survive of us is love.

To the Sea

To step over the low wall that divides
Road from concrete walk above the shore
Brings sharply back something known long before –
The miniature gaiety of seasides.
Everything crowds under the low horizon:
Steep beach, blue water, towels, red bathing caps,
The small hushed waves' repeated fresh collapse
Up the warm yellow sand, and further off
A white steamer stuck in the afternoon –

Still going on, all of it, still going on!
To lie, eat, sleep in hearing of the surf
(Ears to transistors, that sound tame enough
Under the sky), or gently up and down
Lead the uncertain children, frilled in white
And grasping at enormous air, or wheel
The rigid old along for them to feel
A final summer, plainly still occurs
As half an annual pleasure, half a rite,

As when, happy at being on my own,
I searched the sand for Famous Cricketers,
Or, farther back, my parents, listeners
To the same seaside quack, first became known.
Strange to it now, I watch the cloudless scene:
The same clear water over smoothed pebbles,
The distant bathers' weak protesting trebles
Down at its edge, and then the cheap cigars,
The chocolate-papers, tea-leaves, and, between

The rocks, the rusting soup-tins, till the first
Few families start the trek back to the cars.
The white steamer has gone. Like breathed-on glass
The sunlight has turned milky. If the worst
Of flawless weather is our falling short,
It may be that through habit these do best,
Coming to water clumsily undressed
Yearly; teaching their children by a sort
Of clowning; helping the old, too, as they ought.

The Trees

The trees are coming into leaf
Like something almost being said;
The recent buds relax and spread,
Their greenness is a kind of grief.

Is it that they are born again
And we grow old? No, they die too.
Their yearly trick of looking new
Is written down in rings of grain.

Yet still the unresting castles thresh
In fullgrown thickness every May.
Last year is dead, they seem to say,
Begin afresh, afresh, afresh.

Livings

I deal with farmers, things like dips and feed.
Every third month I book myself in at
The —— Hotel in —ton for three days.
The boots carries my lean old leather case
Up to a single, where I hang my hat.
One beer, and then 'the dinner', at which I read
The —*shire Times* from soup to stewed pears.
Births, deaths. For sale. Police court. Motor spares.

Afterwards, whisky in the Smoke Room: Clough,
Margetts, the Captain, Dr. Watterson;
Who makes ends meet, who's taking the knock,
Government tariffs, wages, price of stock.
Smoke hangs under the light. The pictures on
The walls are comic – hunting, the trenches, stuff
Nobody minds or notices. A sound
Of dominoes from the Bar. I stand a round.

Later, the square is empty: a big sky
Drains down the estuary like the bed
Of a gold river, and the Customs House
Still has its office lit. I drowse
Between ex-Army sheets, wondering why
I think it's worthwhile coming. Father's dead:
He used to, but the business now is mine.
It's time for change, in nineteen twenty-nine.

II

Seventy feet down
The sea explodes upwards,
Relapsing, to slaver
Off landing-stage steps –
Running suds, rejoice!

Rocks writhe back to sight.
Mussels, limpets,
Husband their tenacity
In the freezing slither –
Creatures, I cherish you!

By day, sky builds
Grape-dark over the salt
Unsown stirring fields.
Radio rubs its legs,
Telling me of elsewhere:

Barometers falling,
Ports wind-shuttered,
Fleets pent like hounds,
Fires in humped inns
Kippering sea-pictures –

Keep it all off!
By night, snow swerves
(O loose moth world)
Through the stare travelling
Leather-black waters.

Guarded by brilliance
I set plate and spoon,

And after, divining-cards.
Lit shelved liners
Grope like mad worlds westward.

III

Tonight we dine without the Master
(Nocturnal vapours do not please);
The port goes round so much the faster,
Topics are raised with no less ease –
Which advowson looks the fairest,
What the wood from Snape will fetch,
Names for *pudendum mulieris*,
Why is Judas like Jack Ketch?

The candleflames grow thin, then broaden:
Our butler Starveling piles the logs
And sets behind the screen a jordan
(Quicker than going to the bogs).
The wine heats temper and complexion:
Oath-enforced assertions fly
On rheumy fevers, resurrection,
Regicide and rabbit pie.

The fields around are cold and muddy,
The cobbled streets close by are still,
A sizar shivers at his study,
The kitchen cat has made a kill;
The bells discuss the hour's gradations,
Dusty shelves hold prayers and proofs:
Above, Chaldean constellations
Sparkle over crowded roofs.

Forget What Did

Stopping the diary
Was a stun to memory,
Was a blank starting,

One no longer cicatrised
By such words, such actions
As bleakened waking.

I wanted them over,
Hurried to burial
And looked back on

Like the wars and winters
Missing behind the windows
Of an opaque childhood.

And the empty pages?
Should they ever be filled
Let it be with observed

Celestial recurrences,
The day the flowers come,
And when the birds go.

High Windows

When I see a couple of kids
And guess he's fucking her and she's
Taking pills or wearing a diaphragm,
I know this is paradise

Everyone old has dreamed of all their lives –
Bonds and gestures pushed to one side
Like an outdated combine harvester,
And everyone young going down the long slide

To happiness, endlessly. I wonder if
Anyone looked at me, forty years back,
And thought, *That'll be the life;*
No God any more, or sweating in the dark

About hell and that, or having to hide
What you think of the priest. He
And his lot will all go down the long slide
Like free bloody birds. And immediately

Rather than words comes the thought of high windows:
The sun-comprehending glass,
And beyond it, the deep blue air, that shows
Nothing, and is nowhere, and is endless.

Friday Night in the Royal Station Hotel

Light spreads darkly downwards from the high
Clusters of lights over empty chairs
That face each other, coloured differently.
Through open doors, the dining-room declares
A larger loneliness of knives and glass
And silence laid like carpet. A porter reads
An unsold evening paper. Hours pass,
And all the salesmen have gone back to Leeds,
Leaving full ashtrays in the Conference Room.

In shoeless corridors, the lights burn. How
Isolated, like a fort, it is –
The headed paper, made for writing home
(If home existed) letters of exile: *Now
Night comes on. Waves fold behind villages.*

The Old Fools

What do they think has happened, the old fools,
To make them like this? Do they somehow suppose
It's more grown-up when your mouth hangs open and
    drools,
And you keep on pissing yourself, and can't remember
Who called this morning? Or that, if they only chose,
They could alter things back to when they danced
    all night,
Or went to their wedding, or sloped arms some
    September?
Or do they fancy there's really been no change,
And they've always behaved as if they were crippled
    or tight,
Or sat through days of thin continuous dreaming
Watching light move? If they don't (and they can't), it's
    strange:
        Why aren't they screaming?

At death, you break up: the bits that were you
Start speeding away from each other for ever
With no one to see. It's only oblivion, true:
We had it before, but then it was going to end,
And was all the time merging with a unique
    endeavour
To bring to bloom the million-petalled flower
Of being here. Next time you can't pretend
There'll be anything else. And these are the first signs:
Not knowing how, not hearing who, the power
Of choosing gone. Their looks show that they're for it:

Ash hair, toad hands, prune face dried into lines –
    How can they ignore it?

Perhaps being old is having lighted rooms
Inside your head, and people in them, acting.
People you know, yet can't quite name; each looms
Like a deep loss restored, from known doors turning,
Setting down a lamp, smiling from a stair, extracting
A known book from the shelves; or sometimes only
The rooms themselves, chairs and a fire burning,
The blown bush at the window, or the sun's
Faint friendliness on the wall some lonely
Rain-ceased midsummer evening. That is where
    they live:
Not here and now, but where all happened once.
        This is why they give

An air of baffled absence, trying to be there
Yet being here. For the rooms grow farther, leaving
Incompetent cold, the constant wear and tear
Of taken breath, and them crouching below
Extinction's alp, the old fools, never perceiving
How near it is. This must be what keeps them quiet:
The peak that stays in view wherever we go
For them is rising ground. Can they never tell
What is dragging them back, and how it will end?
    Not at night?
Not when the strangers come? Never, throughout
The whole hideous inverted childhood? Well,
        We shall find out.

Going, Going

I thought it would last my time –
The sense that, beyond the town,
There would always be fields and farms,
Where the village louts could climb
Such trees as were not cut down;
I knew there'd be false alarms

In the papers about old streets
And split-level shopping, but some
Have always been left so far;
And when the old part retreats
As the bleak high-risers come
We can always escape in the car.

Things are tougher than we are, just
As earth will always respond
However we mess it about;
Chuck filth in the sea, if you must:
The tides will be clean beyond.
– But what do I feel now? Doubt?

Or age, simply? The crowd
Is young in the M1 café;
Their kids are screaming for more –
More houses, more parking allowed,
More caravan sites, more pay.
On the Business Page, a score

Of spectacled grins approve
Some takeover bid that entails

Five per cent profit (and ten
Per cent more in the estuaries): move
Your works to the unspoilt dales
(Grey area grants)! And when
You try to get near the sea
In summer . . .
                    It seems, just now,
To be happening so very fast;
Despite all the land left free
For the first time I feel somehow
That it isn't going to last,

That before I snuff it, the whole
Boiling will be bricked in
Except for the tourist parts –
First slum of Europe: a role
It won't be so hard to win,
With a cast of crooks and tarts.

And that will be England gone,
The shadows, the meadows, the lanes
The guildhalls, the carved choirs.
There'll be books; it will linger on
In galleries; but all that remains
For us will be concrete and tyres.

Most things are never meant.
This won't be, most likely: but greeds
And garbage are too thick-strewn
To be swept up now, or invent
Excuses that make them all needs.
I just think it will happen, soon.

The Card-Players

Jan van Hogspeuw staggers to the door
And pisses at the dark. Outside, the rain
Courses in cart-ruts down the deep mud lane.
Inside, Dirk Dogstoerd pours himself some more,
And holds a cinder to his clay with tongs,
Belching out smoke. Old Prijck snores with the gale,
His skull face firelit; someone behind drinks ale,
And opens mussels, and croaks scraps of songs
Towards the ham-hung rafters about love.
Dirk deals the cards. Wet century-wide trees
Clash in surrounding starlessness above
This lamplit cave, where Jan turns back and farts,
Gobs at the grate, and hits the queen of hearts.

Rain, wind and fire! The secret, bestial peace!

The Building

Higher than the handsomest hotel
The lucent comb shows up for miles, but see,
All round it close-ribbed streets rise and fall
Like a great sigh out of the last century.
The porters are scruffy; what keep drawing up
At the entrance are not taxis; and in the hall
As well as creepers hangs a frightening smell.

There are paperbacks, and tea at so much a cup,
Like an airport lounge, but those who tamely sit
On rows of steel chairs turning the ripped mags
Haven't come far. More like a local bus,
These outdoor clothes and half-filled shopping bags
And faces restless and resigned, although
Every few minutes comes a kind of nurse

To fetch someone away: the rest refit
Cups back to saucers, cough, or glance below
Seats for dropped gloves or cards. Humans, caught
On ground curiously neutral, homes and names
Suddenly in abeyance; some are young,
Some old, but most at that vague age that claims
The end of choice, the last of hope; and all

Here to confess that something has gone wrong.
It must be error of a serious sort,
For see how many floors it needs, how tall
It's grown by now, and how much money goes
In trying to correct it. See the time,

[63]

Half-past eleven on a working day,
And these picked out of it; see, as they climb

To their appointed levels, how their eyes
Go to each other, guessing; on the way
Someone's wheeled past, in washed-to-rags ward
    clothes:
They see him, too. They're quiet. To realise
This new thing held in common makes them quiet,
For past these doors are rooms, and rooms past those,
And more rooms yet, each one further off

And harder to return from; and who knows
Which he will see, and when? For the moment, wait,
Look down at the yard. Outside seems old enough:
Red brick, lagged pipes, and someone walking by it
Out to the car park, free. Then, past the gate,
Traffic; a locked church; short terraced streets
Where kids chalk games, and girls with hair-dos fetch

Their separates from the cleaners – O world,
Your loves, your chances, are beyond the stretch
Of any hand from here! And so, unreal,
A touching dream to which we all are lulled
But wake from separately. In it, conceits
And self-protecting ignorance congeal
To carry life, collapsing only when

Called to these corridors (for now once more
The nurse beckons –). Each gets up and goes
At last. Some will be out by lunch, or four;
Others, not knowing it, have come to join
The unseen congregations whose white rows

Lie set apart above – women, men;
Old, young; crude facets of the only coin

This place accepts. All know they are going to die.
Not yet, perhaps not here, but in the end,
And somewhere like this. That is what it means,
This clean-sliced cliff; a struggle to transcend
The thought of dying, for unless its powers
Outbuild cathedrals nothing contravenes
The coming dark, though crowds each evening try

With wasteful, weak, propitiatory flowers.

Posterity

Jake Balokowsky, my biographer,
Has this page microfilmed. Sitting inside
His air-conditioned cell at Kennedy
In jeans and sneakers, he's no call to hide
Some slight impatience with his destiny:
'I'm stuck with this old fart at least a year;

I wanted to teach school in Tel Aviv,
But Myra's folks' – he makes the money sign –
'Insisted I got tenure. When there's kids –'
He shrugs. 'It's stinking dead, the research line;
Just let me put this bastard on the skids,
I'll get a couple of semesters leave

To work on Protest Theater.' They both rise,
Make for the Coke dispenser. 'What's he like?
Christ, I just told you. Oh, you know the thing,
That crummy textbook stuff from Freshman Psych,
Not out of kicks or something happening –
One of those old-type *natural* fouled-up guys.'

Dublinesque

Down stucco sidestreets,
Where light is pewter
And afternoon mist
Brings lights on in shops
Above race-guides and rosaries,
A funeral passes.

The hearse is ahead,
But after there follows
A troop of streetwalkers
In wide flowered hats,
Leg-of-mutton sleeves,
And ankle-length dresses.

There is an air of great friendliness,
As if they were honouring
One they were fond of;
Some caper a few steps,
Skirts held skilfully
(Someone claps time),

And of great sadness also.
As they wend away
A voice is heard singing
Of Kitty, or Katy,
As if the name meant once
All love, all beauty.

Homage to a Government

Next year we are to bring the soldiers home
For lack of money, and it is all right.
Places they guarded, or kept orderly,
Must guard themselves, and keep themselves orderly.
We want the money for ourselves at home
Instead of working. And this is all right.

It's hard to say who wanted it to happen,
But now it's been decided nobody minds.
The places are a long way off, not here,
Which is all right, and from what we hear
The soldiers there only made trouble happen.
Next year we shall be easier in our minds.

Next year we shall be living in a country
That brought its soldiers home for lack of money.
The statues will be standing in the same
Tree-muffled squares, and look nearly the same.
Our children will not know it's a different country.
All we can hope to leave them now is money.

1969

This Be The Verse

They fuck you up, your mum and dad.
   They may not mean to, but they do.
They fill you with the faults they had
   And add some extra, just for you.

But they were fucked up in their turn
   By fools in old-style hats and coats,
Who half the time were soppy-stern
   And half at one another's throats.

Man hands on misery to man.
   It deepens like a coastal shelf.
Get out as early as you can,
   And don't have any kids yourself.

How Distant

How distant, the departure of young men
Down valleys, or watching
The green shore past the salt-white cordage
Rising and falling,

Cattlemen, or carpenters, or keen
Simply to get away
From married villages before morning,
Melodeons play

On tiny decks past fraying cliffs of water
Or late at night
Sweet under the differently-swung stars,
When the chance sight

Of a girl doing her laundry in the steerage
Ramifies endlessly.
This is being young,
Assumption of the startled century

Like new store clothes,
The huge decisions printed out by feet
Inventing where they tread,
The random windows conjuring a street.

Sad Steps

Groping back to bed after a piss
I part thick curtains, and am startled by
The rapid clouds, the moon's cleanliness.

Four o'clock: wedge-shadowed gardens lie
Under a cavernous, a wind-picked sky.
There's something laughable about this,

The way the moon dashes through clouds that blow
Loosely as cannon-smoke to stand apart
(Stone-coloured light sharpening the roofs below)

High and preposterous and separate –
Lozenge of love! Medallion of art!
O wolves of memory! Immensements! No,

One shivers slightly, looking up there.
The hardness and the brightness and the plain
Far-reaching singleness of that wide stare

Is a reminder of the strength and pain
Of being young; that it can't come again,
But is for others undiminished somewhere.

Solar

Suspended lion face
Spilling at the centre
Of an unfurnished sky
How still you stand,
And how unaided
Single stalkless flower
You pour unrecompensed.

The eye sees you
Simplified by distance
Into an origin,
Your petalled head of flames
Continuously exploding.
Heat is the echo of your
Gold.

Coined there among
Lonely horizontals
You exist openly.
Our needs hourly
Climb and return like angels.
Unclosing like a hand,
You give for ever.

Annus Mirabilis

Sexual intercourse began
In nineteen sixty-three
(Which was rather late for me) –
Between the end of the *Chatterley* ban
And the Beatles' first LP.

Up till then there'd only been
A sort of bargaining,
A wrangle for a ring,
A shame that started at sixteen
And spread to everything.

Then all at once the quarrel sank:
Everyone felt the same,
And every life became
A brilliant breaking of the bank,
A quite unlosable game.

So life was never better than
In nineteen sixty-three
(Though just too late for me) –
Between the end of the *Chatterley* ban
And the Beatles' first LP.

Vers de Société

My *wife and I have asked a crowd of craps*
To *come and waste their time and ours: perhaps*
You'd care to join us? In a pig's arse, friend.
Day comes to an end.
The gas fire breathes, the trees are darkly swayed.
And so *Dear Warlock-Williams: I'm afraid* –

Funny how hard it is to be alone.
I could spend half my evenings, if I wanted,
Holding a glass of washing sherry, canted
Over to catch the drivel of some bitch
Who's read nothing but *Which*;
Just think of all the spare time that has flown

Straight into nothingness by being filled
With forks and faces, rather than repaid
Under a lamp, hearing the noise of wind,
And looking out to see the moon thinned
To an air-sharpened blade.
A life, and yet how sternly it's instilled

All solitude is selfish. No one now
Believes the hermit with his gown and dish
Talking to God (who's gone too); the big wish
Is to have people nice to you, which means
Doing it back somehow.
Virtue is social. Are, then, these routines

Playing at goodness, like going to church?
Something that bores us, something we don't do well
(Asking that ass about his fool research)
But try to feel, because, however crudely,
It shows us what should be?
Too subtle, that. Too decent, too. Oh hell,

Only the young can be alone freely.
The time is shorter now for company,
And sitting by a lamp more often brings
Not peace, but other things.
Beyond the light stand failure and remorse
Whispering *Dear Warlock-Williams: Why, of course* –

Show Saturday

Grey day for the Show, but cars jam the narrow lanes.
Inside, on the field, judging has started: dogs
(Set their legs back, hold out their tails) and ponies
    (manes
Repeatedly smoothed, to calm heads); over there, sheep
(Cheviot and Blackface); by the hedge, squealing logs
(Chain Saw Competition). Each has its own keen crowd.
In the main arena, more judges meet by a jeep:
The jumping's on next. Announcements, splutteringly
    loud,

Clash with the quack of a man with pound notes round
    his hat
And a lit-up board. There's more than just animals:
Bead-stalls, balloon-men, a Bank; a beer-marquee that
Half-screens a canvas Gents; a tent selling tweed,
And another, jackets. Folks sit about on bales
Like great straw dice. For each scene is linked by spaces
Not given to anything much, where kids scrap, freed,
While their owners stare different ways with incurious
    faces.

The wrestling starts, late; a wide ring of people; then cars;
Then trees; then pale sky. Two young men in acrobats'
    tights
And embroidered trunks hug each other; rock over
    the grass,
Stiff-legged, in a two-man scrum. One falls: they shake
    hands.

[76]

Two more start, one grey-haired: he wins, though.
    They're not so much fights
As long immobile strainings that end in unbalance
With one on his back, unharmed, while the other stands
Smoothing his hair. But there are other talents –

The long high tent of growing and making, wired-off
Wood tables past which crowds shuffle, eyeing the
    scrubbed spaced
Extrusions of earth: blanch leeks like church candles,
    six pods of
Broad beans (one split open), dark shining-leafed
    cabbages – rows
Of single supreme versions, followed (on laced
Paper mats) by dairy and kitchen; four brown eggs,
    four white eggs,
Four plain scones, four dropped scones, pure
    excellences that enclose
A recession of skills. And, after them, lambing-sticks,
    rugs,

Needlework, knitted caps, baskets, all worthy, all
    well done,
But less than the honeycombs. Outside, the jumping's
    over.
The young ones thunder their ponies in competition
Twice round the ring; then trick races, Musical Stalls,
Sliding off, riding bareback, the ponies dragged to and
    fro for
Bewildering requirements, not minding. But now, in the
    background,
Like shifting scenery, horse-boxes move; each crawls
Towards the stock entrance, tilting and swaying, bound

For far-off farms. The pound-note man decamps.
The car park has thinned. They're loading jumps on a
    truck.
Back now to private addresses, gates and lamps
In high stone one-street villages, empty at dusk,
And side roads of small towns (sports finals stuck
In front doors, allotments reaching down to the
    railway);
Back now to autumn, leaving the ended husk
Of summer that brought them here for Show Saturday –

The men with hunters, dog-breeding wool-defined
    women,
Children all saddle-swank, mugfaced middleaged wives
Glaring at jellies, husbands on leave from the garden
Watchful as weasels, car-tuning curt-haired sons –
Back now, all of them, to their local lives:
To names on vans, and business calendars
Hung up in kitchens; back to loud occasions
In the Corn Exchange, to market days in bars,

To winter coming, as the dismantled Show
Itself dies back into the area of work.
Let it stay hidden there like strength, below
Sale-bills and swindling; something people do,
Not noticing how time's rolling smithy-smoke
Shadows much greater gestures; something they share
That breaks ancestrally each year into
Regenerate union. Let it always be there.

Money

Quarterly, is it, money reproaches me:
   'Why do you let me lie here wastefully?
I am all you never had of goods and sex.
   You could get them still by writing a few cheques.'

So I look at others, what they do with theirs:
   They certainly don't keep it upstairs.
By now they've a second house and car and wife:
   Clearly money has something to do with life

– In fact, they've a lot in common, if you enquire:
   You can't put off being young until you retire,
And however you bank your screw, the money you save
   Won't in the end buy you more than a shave.

I listen to money singing. It's like looking down
   From long french windows at a provincial town,
The slums, the canal, the churches ornate and mad
   In the evening sun. It is intensely sad.

Cut Grass

Cut grass lies frail:
Brief is the breath
Mown stalks exhale.
Long, long the death

It dies in the white hours
Of young-leafed June
With chestnut flowers,
With hedges snowlike strewn,

White lilac bowed,
Lost lanes of Queen Anne's lace,
And that high-builded cloud
Moving at summer's pace.

Love

The difficult part of love
Is being selfish enough,
Is having the blind persistence
To upset an existence
Just for your own sake.
What cheek it must take.

And then the unselfish side –
How can you be satisfied,
Putting someone else first
So that you come off worst?
My life is for me.
As well ignore gravity.

Still, vicious or virtuous,
Love suits most of us.
Only the bleeder found
Selfish this wrong way round
Is ever wholly rebuffed,
And he can get stuffed.

The Life with a Hole in it

When I throw back my head and howl
People (women mostly) say
But you've always done what you want,
You always get your own way
– A perfectly vile and foul
Inversion of all that's been.
What the old ratbags mean
Is I've never done what I don't.

So the shit in the shuttered château
Who does his five hundred words
Then parts out the rest of the day
Between bathing and booze and birds
Is far off as ever, but so
Is that spectacled schoolteaching sod
(Six kids, and the wife in pod,
And her parents coming to stay) . . .

Life is an immobile, locked,
Three-handed struggle between
Your wants, the world's for you, and (worse)
The unbeatable slow machine
That brings what you'll get. Blocked,
They strain round a hollow stasis
Of havings-to, fear, faces.
Days sift down it constantly. Years.

Aubade

I work all day, and get half-drunk at night.
Waking at four to soundless dark, I stare.
In time the curtain-edges will grow light.
Till then I see what's really always there:
Unresting death, a whole day nearer now,
Making all thought impossible but how
And where and when I shall myself die.
Arid interrogation: yet the dread
Of dying, and being dead,
Flashes afresh to hold and horrify.

The mind blanks at the glare. Not in remorse
– The good not done, the love not given, time
Torn off unused – nor wretchedly because
An only life can take so long to climb
Clear of its wrong beginnings, and may never;
But at the total emptiness for ever,
The sure extinction that we travel to
And shall be lost in always. Not to be here,
Not to be anywhere,
And soon; nothing more terrible, nothing more true.

This is a special way of being afraid
No trick dispels. Religion used to try,
That vast moth-eaten musical brocade
Created to pretend we never die,
And specious stuff that says *No rational being
Can fear a thing it will not feel*, not seeing
That this is what we fear – no sight, no sound,

No touch or taste or smell, nothing to think with,
Nothing to love or link with,
The anaesthetic from which none come round.

And so it stays just on the edge of vision,
A small unfocused blur, a standing chill
That slows each impulse down to indecision.
Most things may never happen: this one will,
And realisation of it rages out
In furnace-fear when we are caught without
People or drink. Courage is no good:
It means not scaring others. Being brave
Lets no one off the grave.
Death is no different whined at than withstood.

Slowly light strengthens, and the room takes shape.
It stands plain as a wardrobe, what we know,
Have always known, know that we can't escape,
Yet can't accept. One side will have to go.
Meanwhile telephones crouch, getting ready to ring
In locked-up offices, and all the uncaring
Intricate rented world begins to rouse.
The sky is white as clay, with no sun.
Work has to be done.
Postmen like doctors go from house to house.

The Mower

The mower stalled, twice; kneeling, I found
A hedgehog jammed up against the blades,
Killed. It had been in the long grass.

I had seen it before, and even fed it, once.
Now I had mauled its unobtrusive world
Unmendably. Burial was no help:

Next morning I got up and it did not.
The first day after a death, the new absence
Is always the same; we should be careful

Of each other, we should be kind
While there is still time.

Letter to a Friend about Girls

After comparing lives with you for years
I see how I've been losing: all the while
I've met a different gauge of girl from yours.
Grant that, and all the rest makes sense as well:
My mortification at your pushovers,
Your mystification at my fecklessness –
Everything proves we play in separate leagues.
Before, I couldn't credit your intrigues
Because I thought all girls the same, but yes,
You bag real birds, though they're from alien covers.

Now I believe your staggering skirmishes
In train, tutorial and telephone booth,
The wife whose husband watched away matches
While she behaved so badly in a bath,
And all the rest who beckon from that world
Described on Sundays only, where to want
Is straightway to be wanted, seek to find,
And no one gets upset or seems to mind
At what you say to them, or what you don't:
A world where all the nonsense is annulled,

And beauty is accepted slang for yes.
But equally, haven't you noticed mine?
They have their world, not much compared with yours,
But where they work, and age, and put off men
By being unattractive, or too shy,
Or having morals – anyhow, none give in:
Some of them go quite rigid with disgust

At anything but marriage: that's all lust
And so not worth considering; they begin
Fetching your hat, so that you have to lie

Till everything's confused: you mine away
For months, both of you, till the collapse comes
Into remorse, tears, and wondering why
You ever start such boring barren games
– But there, don't mind my *saeva indignatio*:
I'm happier now I've got things clear, although
It's strange we never meet each other's sort:
There should be equal chances, I'd've thought.
Must finish now. One day perhaps I'll know
What makes you be so lucky in your ratio

– One of those 'more things', could it be? *Horatio*.

December 1959

Love Again

Love again: wanking at ten past three
(Surely he's taken her home by now?),
The bedroom hot as a bakery,
The drink gone dead, without showing how
To meet tomorrow, and afterwards,
And the usual pain, like dysentery.

Someone else feeling her breasts and cunt,
Someone else drowned in that lash-wide stare,
And me supposed to be ignorant,
Or find it funny, or not to care,
Even . . . but why put it into words?
Isolate rather this element

That spreads through other lives like a tree
And sways them on in a sort of sense
And say why it never worked for me.
Something to do with violence
A long way back, and wrong rewards,
And arrogant eternity.

20 September 1979

Index of Titles and First Lines